Dear Hot Flash Gal

Every Answer to a Gal's Every Question

Photos by Kelly Povo
Words by Phyllis Root & Kelly Povo

CONARI PRESS

First published in 2005 by Conari Press,
an imprint of Red Wheel/Weiser, LLC
York Beach, ME
With offices at:
368 Congress Street
Boston, MA 02210
www.redwheelweiser.com

ISBN 1-57324-257-8

Typeset in Shmelvetica by Kathleen Wilson Fivel
Printed in China
Everbest
12 11 10 09 08 07 06 05
   8 7 6 5 4 3 2 1

Hey, all you menopausal missies—
Feeling hot? Hopeless?
Are you huffing? Hanging low?

Have no fear—
Hot Flash Gal is here!

Dear Hot Flash Gal,

I'm too hot to handle. How can I keep cool?

Signed,
Frying in Frisco

Dear Frying,

There are bad ways to be cool,

And good ways to be cool.

Try a squeezy
from someone freezy.

Stay wet. No sweat.

Every hot flash is
just a cheap tropical vacation.

—Sincerely,
Hot Flash Gal

P.S. Remember, always serve
your drinks on the rocks.

Dear Hot Flash Gal,

Help! I can't get down like I used to.

Signed,
Aching in Akron

Dear Aching,
Getting down isn't all it's cracked up to be.

If you can't get down, get up.

Start with very
low impact aerobics.

Work up to weight lifting.

And be sure to load up on carbs.

—Sincerely,
Hot Flash Gal

P.S. Remember, keep
moving and grooving.

Dear Hot Flash Gal,

Nobody lights my fire. How can I find a good match?

Signed,
Drying up in Detroit Lakes

Dear Drying Up,

Don't despair. You're still a great catch!

And you don't have to settle
for cheap, cheap sex.

Go for the guy with buns of steel.

Just make sure he's in touch
with his feminine side,

won't melt,

and has more facial hair than you do.

—Sincerely,
Hot Flash Gal

P.S. Remember, don't be phony,
just be yourself!

Dear Hot Flash Gal,

My spirits are lower than my boobs!
How can I get a lift?

Signed,
Drooping in Dismal, TN

Dear Drooping,

Try a new attitude.

Turn over a new leaf.

Travel.

Take
risks.

Laugh till they ask you to leave.

—Sincerely,
Hot Flash Gal

P.S. Sure, you're
going through some
monumental changes.

But take a tip from Hot Flash Gal.

You're so hot you're cool!

When not answering questions about broken a/c units, Kelly Povo and Phyllis Root keep busy writing books. They collaborated on Hot Flash Gal and Gladys on the Go. Kelly has her own greeting card line (visit her at www.kellycards.com) and Phyllis also writes children's books.